MY NAGGING DAY
BOOK TWO

Ah yes Lesotho, South Africa
What can I say apart from:
You are a rare beauty
You are a part of the womb
The womb of Africa – Mama Africa
Lesotho you are the true meaning of the south
You are the South – South Africa

Michelle Jean

Ah man Good God this book is so close to the next one but it cannot be helped.

This book won't be as long as the first because I am hoping to just talk about one thing.

Lately you've been showing me so many things that pertains to me and I truly thank you because I infinitely know that you are truly there for me.

As I've said before, if you cannot forgive a man in the living you cannot forgive him in death and this is so right – true.

I've been through a lot at the hands of evil hence the book Behind the Scars. This book I cannot finish hence it's tucked away. I don't even want to look at it hence Behind the Scars has and have become my forbidden book. I will not edit it. I refuse to hence it stays as is with all its mistakes – verb confusion and spelling errors.

This book is not even the tip of the iceberg of what I went through at the hands of physical and spiritual evil. This is why I tell young children this:

If you have a good parent that care for you, treat you right and want what's best for you, do not give her or him (your parent or parents) up to follow in the footsteps of evil.

Evil and wicked people are just that, wicked and evil. They have no part and parcel in Good God's abode hence they make others suffer in the living. Hell's fire is there abode and trust me infinitely on this. **<u>EVIL AND WICKED PEOPLE WILL BURN IN HELL FOR THE EVILS THAT THEY DO ON EARTH. THERE IS NO ESCAPING THE JUDGEMENT OF DEATH. HENCE THE WAGES OF SIN IS DEATH.</u>**

Do not let evil and wicked people – friends take you out of your good home to join them.

Do not let them coheres you into doing something that you do not want to do because when trouble comes you are the one to be left holding the bag.

Evil run from its lies and danger. So do not let anyone put you or your family in danger – harm's way. At the end of the day you are going to be the one to pay in hell.

Yes they will pay but you will pay more because you know better hence you are to do better.

Yes I am still facing hell because it seems some of my children want to learn the hard way and trust me I am standing aside. All I am waiting on is for Good God to open a way for me so that I can leave this land.

I truly need him to find me a good and true home in South Africa because my homeland is not clean. He's also shown me the nastiness of the people in a dream

– vision. My homeland became clean but my own set me up to fall hence I know that none are with Good God. They prefer evil over good so I refuse to plead to Good God for none. Let them come out of their own messes themselves.

Good God showed me the beauty and rebirth of the land and still for all they are going to set me up. They the people did this to Peter Tosh, Paul Bogle, Bob Marley and more importantly Marcus Mosiah Garvey. So what say me? I am no different. Hence I will not defend them in this harvest. Let them bloody well suffer.

All this stems from jealousy. Many will be jealous but it matters to me not the jealousy. With many of us, it's why did God have to choose her? Why couldn't he choose me?

And like I will tell everyone:

When you start living clean
When you start trusting Good God

When you stop cheating on your spouse
When you stop lying
When you stop cheating on your taxes
When you stop living in sin
When you start talking right, walking right and living right amongst other things then Good God will choose you.

If Good God cannot trust you he cannot use you.

Truth and trust is key to Good God. Just as how you want people to trust you. Good God need to trust you also.

Remember Allelujah. Well this is the name the spirit cries out to in the living. Hence the true name of Good God is Allelujah. Both good and evil cry out to Allelujah which is the true breath of life.

I told you my homeland had the truth but because of lies they polluted the name and land of God – Good God. Hence they have become unclean in the eyes and sight of Good God.

We got to that stage. God – Good God have never deemed anyone unclean in my lifetime until now.

My homeland – Jamaica has become unclean. Do you know how hurtful it is to hear Good God say Jamaica is unclean?

<u>We the Jamaican people have disappointed Good God. He didn't say Iceland, he didn't say Africa, he didn't say Greenland, he didn't say Nod of all places, he didn't say Iraq or Iran; he said Jamaica is unclean.</u>

This is the place of my birth. Yes I don't live there because he took me out of there when I was a child. But still for all Jamaica is dear to me because it is the place of my birth and my own people caused the land including the name of God to become unclean.

Like I said, we had the breath of life and let it go hence we no longer have ALLELUJAH.

Jamaica has an opportunity to become clean but like I said, she, that one woman is going to set me up to fall hence Jamaica – the people of Jamaica will revert back to their dirty ways.

Am I shocked?

Nothing shocks me when it comes to Jamaica because like I said, young children are being slaughtered like pigs and discarded at road side like hogs and the scumbag government does nothing about it.

Neither JLP nor PNP care so nothing surprises me.

Yes you can want better for people but if people do not want better for self then truly leave them alone.

This is why I tell Good God that I refuse to plea for the people of my homeland because I truly know their wickedness.

So Good God, I am coming to you yet again and I am going to nag you until I get this. I told you no hitchers and this goes for Jamaica also.

Before evil rise again in Jamaica shut evil the hell down infinitely and indefinitely. I am tired of evil destroying our good land. The people of Jamaica did not make Jamaica you did. You had no right to allow demons to cause your land to become unclean. The land of Nod have done vile acts in your eyes and you've not deemed them unclean but you've deemed my homeland unclean and for this I don't think I can forgive you. Yes I know Nod is unclean but you did not tell me they were. You said Jamaica is unclean.

I specifically told you I wanted to enjoy you in Jamaica and now I can't and I am bent. Yes I am upset. Help me to clean the land up but in doing so give evil and wicked people their eviction notice. Let them truly flee the island because I do not want nor do I need any wicked people there. Black people have and has been disappointing you for centuries let the disappointment stop. You cannot continue to hold out for us to change. You showed me the vision that someone is going to set me up after Jamaica came back to. What you are telling me is that my people do not want good for themselves so kick them the bleep off the island now. Do not give them a bleeping home because I give you my word I will never forgive you if this happens. I don't care where on this planet (earth or otherwise) this set up is. I will never forgive you if it happens because you knew before hand hence you showed me before it happens. Only let true, good and clean people stay on the island come on now.

It's about time you take a hard stance with us. I don't care who it is. It could be me. Take a damned hard stance now man. Come on now.

Why the hell should Jamaica be cleaned up and you allow nasty people to come back and dirty it? No. I refuse to let nasty people come back and dirty the island. Before so sink it backside. I refuse evil and the hitchers that come along for the ride. If you cannot keep the place clean then what point is it to keep the island standing?

No I am not preeing death but why should evil come back in a clean place. Why should evil come back and destroy what we have tried so hard to fix? Look at the way I cuss my people for them to smarten up and do better. Come on now. No evil must be allowed back on the island (Jamaica). Come on now. What are you telling me? All is in vain?

Why clean it (the island) in the first place for evil and wicked people to come back and dirty it. Mi did tell yu sey mi like evil?

Mi did tell you sey mi waane commune with evil and his people?

No come on now Good God. Do better because evil is not for me or you.

Let me get off track here now.

Duly remember BEHIND THE SCARS. You know as well as saw the hell I went through at the hands of this demon. No one has been though hell like I've been through hell because this book does not fully detail the hell I went through at the hands of this man. My life was not worth it hence he did all to me. This is why I say if you cannot forgive a man in the living you cannot forgive him in death. <u>And I Michelle Jean give you my more than forever ever truth that I would never forgive him for what he did to me and my children.</u> I did not have to go through what he put me through. My children did not have to go through what he put them through. I remember it all and trust me Good God not even you can make me forgive him. <u>**Any day you say Michelle forgive him for what he has done to me I give you my word of truth that I**</u>

would infinitely and indefinitely walk away from you.

You took me out of hell.

I was literally in hell.

I was bound in hell with a noose – a shackle around my neck. I remembered the man that loose me. He ate the 4 worms that held me captive. So no one can come and tell me to walk away from you Good God because I know what I came out of. I refuse to be ungrateful and untrue to you. I will walk with you until the end. All when yu a shake mi off yu feet dem mi still a clutch and cling on worse than crazy glue.

Good God me to be ungrateful to you after mi a no idiat. Mi a fool?

Remember when I was almost on the streets in the dead of winter because I got evicted out of my apartment. Remember the offerings of Satan and the way he cast doubt on you for me to accept him and his offerings.

<u>I did not accept him or his offerings.</u> I stayed true to you hence I nagged you to get a job because of my financial difficulties. Hence today I can lift my hands to your glory and say my life is a little bit easier financially **<u>BECAUSE OF YOU AND ONLY YOU.</u>** I cannot complain about my finances. All I can complain to you about is my vacation. I need to take a vacation and I want and need to go back to the Mother Land which is South Africa. I have to meet you there hence I refuse to turn from you.

Like I said, I will not forgive this man because of the evils he has and have done to me in the living as well as in death.

Good God, he told me he was sorry for the pain he caused me. He's bleeping too late. Like I said, I will never forgive him for what he did to me in the living and in death.

No one truly knows hence I tell people if you don't know about the spiritual world shut the bleep up. Say nothing because who feels it knows it.

He tried to kill me in the living and in death. Hence people talk a lot of crap in the living. They don't know that evil walks and some evil do sleep with humans.

Evil do have sex with some humans but to tell people this they laugh.

<u>Evil is heavy – hence we say dead weight.</u>

<u>The body is light but the spirit is heavy and no one can carry the weight of the dead.</u> Just look at the Atlas with the weight of the world on his shoulder. Although he was not real but dead weight is heavier than this.

Yu think a likkle sinting dis man do to mi inna death?

No one has control over the evil death that's why some obeah man and woman use the dead in their nastiness.

Hence nastiness will not stop because the hearts and mind of humans are evil – belongs to evil – wicked.

Now this creep – evil dead a come roune mi again. This time I was in the bank working. I had two books editing. My books. One of gold and black but the other one I cannot remember the colour. But you know what I am so not going to get into this dream – the bank scene because I saw the inverted triangle in the bank. The inverted triangle was at the feet of this teller. Meaning the chair she was sitting on, underneath it was an inverted triangle hence her life has been turned down. So Good God I don't know if someone wants her job and has turned her down but she was sitting on an inverted triangle. And yes she is Spanish. I don't know what Spanish country she is from but she has been turned down.

Onwards I go.

It was lunchtime so I collected my things to take my lunch about 1 pm not noon. So the go I go outside the bank to find my car it was not there. I knew who took my car. It was that demon duppy that took my car. It was parked in the back row of the parking lot and he was in the back seat sort of lying down. The windows were down somewhat but he could not come out of the car. The car was broken down – overheating from the back and you could see the smoke or steam. I did not go in the car because there was a white gentleman at the back of the car. He was trying to fix the car I think because he said something about he's the one that did this. He asked me if I wanted to go into his van like bus but I said no because the tires of his van like bus were low. The van like bus look broken down. So I went on my way *leaving this demon duppy in is overheated car – brown on brown car.*

Hence I am coming to you yet again Good God and I am truly going to vent. What part of not seeing this man do you not comprehend? I do not want this man around me. This is not the first time he's coming around me with smokeless fire. He's done this before and I am fed up of it. I know he's in hell and I refuse to take him out.

Leave him the hell in hell because I refuse to let him loose. Keep his bleeping ass buried in hell forever ever. I will not be his saving grace. I refuse to because he tried to turn my children against me and in many ways he turned my daughter against me. Hence there is no forgiveness for him when it comes to me. I refuse to forgive him and nothing that he tries will make me forgive him. I told you Good God to take hold of my good spirit and keep it in your good care and you are ignoring me. My spirit should be good and true to you also. I told you I have to be true and good to you all around and you are not listening and I am getting pissed off at you.

My good spirit is mine because you gave it to me and it is cherished. I told you I have no control of it in the spiritual realm because the spiritual realm is that powerful hence I trust you to keep it safe.

Now as for this man. Let it be over now because I am not dicking around when it comes to him.

Bleep him forever ever.

I will not rescue him in hell and you cannot make me rescue him. I infinitely refuse to. If I accept his apology and rescue him than I would have to rescue Satan and all the evil and wicked people of hell and I will not do that. So please do not let my spirit go against my good and true will. I do not do it to you so don't do it to me because it's not fair. I nag you for goodness and truth not evil. Evil know and *knows what they are doing and I cannot forgive willful sin – willful evil. I will not beg for any evil person at the appointed or last hour. It could be my children, I will not beg for them period. Do not go against me for this Good God because you will be violating me and I do not violate you in that way.*

You cannot make me go against my spiritual and physical will because I need them to be on the same accord. I need my spirit to be strong as well as fully and truly guarded against all forms of spiritual and physical evil.

I cannot have you going against my good and true will Good God.

This man come again with fire – smoke.

He's burning in hell and mi fi save him after what he did to me in the living. Step aside now Good God.

No truly step aside and mek mi handle this.

Death you si di fire inna hell wey surround dis man.

No death you step the hell aside because you are crap – shit compared to greater death.

Greater death. You listen to me and listen to me keenly. Do not deviate from my good desire – will.

You have the keys to the pits of hell hence this is my true will and need of you.

Hear me now because I did tell Good God I will never forgive this man for what he did to me. So end it now!!!!!

Keep this piece of deadlef and dead weight wey drangcrow no want away from me. No even cungoworm want him because he literally stinks wuse dan shit.

I do not care how hot you have to make his pit in hell for him to stay away from me. Do it and keep him the hell away from me.

We have nothing in common nor do we have anything in the living or spiritual together. I've committed myself and my children including the ones I had with him to Good God and Good Life. So keep him away from us. He is infinitely and indefinitely banned from terrorizing me and humanity. He was a liar and deceiver just like Satan hence lock him away like you've done Satan. No one must loose him. Anyone lose him must and will have hell to pay. Use you damned key and lock him up infinitely and indefinitely forever ever because I will not defile Good God for him.

I will not forgive him hence I do not want him violating my personal space as well as private space.

Good God I am trusting you to ensure greater death follow my command – instructions. Like I said, if it takes the heat and fire of infinite atoms – atomic fire to keep this demon at bay then let it be so. I will not disrespect you for him or anyone.

He knew what he was doing in the living hence humanity knows that the life they live on earth determines where they go in the afterlife.

I do not play when it comes to me and you Good God and no one should violate my good and true space with you.

My children are our children and they are sacred to me. But it does not mean when the time has come for us to leave this land and they are not ready I won't leave their asses behind.

I will leave them because when you say move we have to move.

When you say go we have to go and it matters not who or what we leave behind. We have to go.

Like I said, my true love for you is beyond words and there are times when this truth and true love overflows. The energy and feel is so wonderful and beautiful that you want to touch someone for them to feel what you feel.

I will not give you up do you hear me!!!!!!!

I refuse to hence close all doors to evil globally on an infinite and indefinite forever ever scale.

No Good God. I don't want evil to get to me and you. Why the hell should evil continue to pollute me and you? Keep me from you.

Evil destroy and I refuse to let any evil destroy you and what you have given me.

I need to enjoy you.

I need to come back home and be at true peace and rest with you.

You are more than my hope so why should I let evil come in yet again? Mi a fool? Mi noa di danger of evil so keep evil at bay.

In so doing, protect and guard my children from all evil. I know if people can't set me up they will try to set up my children hence I am relying on you to protect them in every way.

Keep them safe because I did commit and dedicate them into your good care and good service. Yes I know it was after they were born but I still committed them to your good care.

Anyone that is going to set us up let the set up fall right back on them. Be my forever ever postage that says return to sender when it comes to all evil.

Yes you are my return postage in the spiritual realm as well as in the physical realm. Not just for me but for my children and the good seeds you have given me.

Good God, no one must come between me and you.

So mi no noa wey dis creebay creebay dry out rotten bone wey stinka dan all di demons of hell combined no lef mi di bleep alone?

Dis literal gutta belly wus dan smell bad unclean beast wey wussara unclean dan the land and people of Jamaica no lef mi di bleep alone?

Babylonian stench including the stench of sin smell betta dan him. Wey di BC and RC im no stop badda mi?

Im ha mine and ambition?

I forget im inna hell cause not even Satan and Sin ha ambition das why dem linga around.

No Good God, dis reeve out sketell wey di demons inna hell a use literally fi lef mi alone.

Evil dead nuffi mingle with clean and decent people. Hence Good God do your job and lock off the evil dead because the time frame of sin is infinitely over.

This is your time God – Good God, so use it wisely and issue every form of sin and evil in physical and spiritual realm their walking papers. Meaning none must be left on earth.

No form of evil including wicked and sinful – deceitful humans as well must be left on earth.

Like I said, I need to enjoy you and I cannot do that with evil around.

This is our time Good God so let us shine in a good way and replenish the earth. Meaning clean it up in a good and true way.

Mother Earth must be clean and tidy hence we must be infinitely clean and tidy.

No paper or garbage must be in our lands. We must have recycling depots and incinerators for garbage.

Good God, I so don't want or need us to bury our garbage in the earth. It's plain out nasty. That's all I got to say.

We have to be clean.

But Good God this demon bright eeee?

Who the hell is he to think I would violate you by saving him?

Did he ever think of what he did to me and my family?

Did he ever think about the pain he caused me?

Did he ever think about the lies he told me?

Did he ever think of how he caused me to hurt you?

Did he ever think of the pain he caused you?

Damn bright. Afterall.

Michelle Jean

God it's almost four o'clock in the morning and I cannot sleep.

My internal clock is once again in sync with the autumn months.

The weather is getting chilly at nights hence little sleep.

Funny the 2:55 a.m. wake up time and the next to impossible sleep – going back to sleep.

Yes I have to bug you since I cannot go back to sleep.

Body hot but I cannot turn on the fan because I don't think the fan can cool me down.

Ah well such is life when you are Michelle Jean.

So God – Good God because I am awake I am going to wake you.

I would truly love to go for a walk but I so do not want to walk the road so late at night.

I so wish I had a house with a home gym for nights like these. Yes the exercise regime.

Pity but that's the way life is sometimes.

It's just me and you Good God so wake up and spend some quality time with me.

Michelle Jean
September 10, 2013

Yes I cannot sleep and I so need company.

Good God wake up and let me nag you because I cannot sleep.

GOOOOOOOD wake up I can't sleep. It's 4 o'clock in the morning. Come spend some quality time with me.

The apartment is quiet but the road – outside is noisy.

Cars – vehicles driving on the road.

I thought night time was meant for sleep.

No wonder earth is the way it is. Too much vehicles on the road at nights.

When do people have time for family?

Ah well to each his own hence I am up nagging you.

Are you up yet?

Where's my vacation to the south? South Africa.

God I'm going to nag you this morning.

Where's my trip to South Africa?

GOOOOOOD, I want to go to South Africa. Where's my trip?

Tell me something Good God, how can I meet you in the womb of life – the cradle of life when I have no financial means to get there?

I have no BBJ nor do I have a Gulfstream 550. This is your fault hence I am bugging you.

Yes I can blame you.

GOOOOD – Good God where is our private jet?

I need to meet you in the womb of life. I need to get there hence I am bothering you for my good vacation which is our good vacation.

Michelle Jean

God – Good God wake up! I am nudging you. I want to go to South Africa and since I cannot go home I am infinitely going to nag you.

GOOOOOD – Good God am I getting to you?

Am I pissing you off yet?

Where's my vacation – my home in South Africa?

Where's my plane ticket because I am bored of North America and since I cannot go home to Jamaica you owe me an awesome vacation.

GOOOOOD – Good God am I bugging you yet? Wake up! You need to get up and prepare your private jet. You need to take me to South Africa. I will not settle for a commercial airline. I need to fly in your personal plane – private jet.

GOOOOOD – Good God you're late. Because I'm still waiting on you – your good private jet.

GOOOOOD I need a vacation.

Am I bugging you yet?

Wake up because Africa is calling me and you.

GOOOOOD are we there yet?

No we're not because I am still here.

GOOOOOD I am going to bug you until you give me my need and that's a trip – a good and fantastic trip to South Africa with that special someone. Preferably you.

GOOOOD – Good God where is my trip to South Africa.

Michelle Jean

Good – Good God it's early in the morning and since I can't sleep, I am so going to fatigue and nag you.

Come on no smiling because you know the nag I can be so cave in and give me my heart's desire – need. I refuse to go to anyone else hence I am coming to you.

Where's my good vacation in South Africa Good God?

GOOOOOOOOOOOOOOOOOD I need you. Where's my good vacation with you?

I cannot bug anyone but you hence I am nagging you.

It's after 4 am in the morning and I need you hence I am calling out to you as well as nagging you.

I do not have a bed partner apart from you. Well you're my bed but that's not the point. I need a vacation and I am so coming to you for it – nagging you.

You know I can't do without you and nagging you. And since I cannot sleep I am so waking you – bugging you.

If I can't sleep you can't sleep hence I am nagging you.

I know, I know I'm a pain but I can't help it. It's the way I am with you.

GOOOOD are you up yet?

Am I truly nagging you?

I know I am but truly see with me because I'm bored. I can't sleep hence I'm nagging you.

So take me on a vacation with you because I yearn to be free – alone with you.

I want to climb the highest mountain with you.

I want to bathe in the nicest waterfall.

I want to call out your name in glee and say Good GOOOOOOOOOOD I truly love you.

I want to truly dance with Fight This Feeling by Shaggy and Beres Hammond with you. Yes forget George Clooney. He's so out of my good books for the time being.

Yes I know it seems like I am using you but would never do that to you.

I need you to bring your boasy self and we can light up the universe together with the brightness of our good and true stars.

I want to jump on your back and say God – Good God will you carry me?

Yes I'll bat my eyes too. So GOOOOOD – Good God can I go on vacation with you?

Michelle Jean

I know I am bothersome Good God but who else do you have to nag you?

Yes I know it's early but I can't sleep. I have to nag someone and who better to nag than you?

Ah if only I had a telephone number for you?

No wait scrap that. My writings like these are our telephone. Well my telephone anyway.

So God – Good God truly see with me because this is my nagging day – book two.

I don't know Good God because my nights are getting lonely.

It's a pity you could not sit by my bedside and sing me a sweet lullaby.

I am wide awake so I truly have to wake you and talk to you.

Do you truly love me?

Are you truly with me?

Do you truly care about me?

Am I your favorite one and all your favorite one and only?

And it's not say what!

Am I your favorite one and all your favorite one and only?

Well don't answer that at least not yet because I've just put you on the spot.

But truly am I your favorite one and all your favorite one and only?

I so need to know.

Hopefully one day you will let me know.

Michelle

Yes Good God I am hot.

Why does my body have to overheat so much especially my back?

Good God where's my vitamins and minerals because the body is changing.

No I don't think they are hot flashes because I still get a regular menstrual.

Yes I'm starting to miss a month here and there but not on the regular.

Instead of getting 13+ periods for the year it's now down to 12 for some strange reason. But don't quote me because I've truly not counted the exact amount of periods I get in one year. But I know I am missing one or two.

Yes the body is hot but I guess that's life when the body no longer requires the egg – ovulation.

Michelle Jean

Ah Good God permanently cool my body down.

Be the light cool breeze that I need on my back daily.

Good God not too cold but just right – the right temperature.

Good God can you be my good child?

No that cannot be because you are God – Good God.

Ah well I am crazy because look at it Good God. I asked you to be my child.

Weird by true. I did ask hence please do not charge me for sin or hold this question against me. If I've passed my place, truly forgive me but it's one of those weird moments where I truly have to be me.

Ah well, I asked but I know it cannot be because you are truly God – Good God alone.

Michelle Jean

Yes I've stopped bugging you Good God. It's 4:52 a.m. and I think I should go mop the floor.

I need to tire out my body.

Better yet the sun will be up soon. Maybe I should go hand wash and stop bothering you so much.

I have a lot of dirty laundry to do and you know how I truly love to hand wash.

I have my Linda Soap and Snuggle. Have to use Snuggle because I think this is the fabric softener you want me to use continually. Yes I saw it before me hence I cannot stray from it. I have to use it.

Fleecy is nice but I have to use Snuggle hence I use it because like I said, it was the one I saw before me literally.

Michelle Jean

Ah God – Good God what are we going to do today. I need to hand wash, are you going to help me?

Well you can make me breakfast lunch and dinner.

I know I have to clean. I need to wipe the walls and get them cleaner.

I have to clean the stove.

Man oh man, the grease on the walls.

Got to get me some Spray Nine. Hopefully that will work.

Got to keep my place clean despite the kids.

Yes they're in school except for one. Yes I want to kick him out because he has no ambition at all when it comes to going to school.

Michelle Jean

Yes God – Good God I've nagged you.
It's 5:01 am and I am still writing strong.

Gone are the days of sleeping through the night.

It's getting cold hence the sleepless and restless nights.

I don't even think it would matter if I had someone sharing my bed because I would get truly bored of him and kick him out of my bed.

No for real Good God. You know how I am when it comes to seeing the face of people day in and day out. You get tired of them. Well me at least. I want to miss you and besides I like being alone in some ways but in others I don't.

I guess deep down I don't want or need someone to come into my life and take me from you.

Yes I am scared because you are sacred to me.

The relationship we have is special to me and I so do not want that to change.

I infinitely have to have my Good God time on days like these.

Good God you are precious to me hence I do not want or need anyone to change me.

I am more than infinitely set in my ways when it comes to you and me.

Hence no changes are allowed when it comes to me and you.

Michelle Jean

Good God I so do not want to let you go but I have to say goodnight. Well it's good morning.

Truly have some roast breadfruit, ackee and saltfish and Jamaican chocolate tea with cinnamon for me and you.

My body is getting tired now hence I have to bid you adieu.

I need to get some sleep.

My brain needs rest hence I am getting disoriented in thought.

Confused in writing. Hence the body must rest.

The spirit must sleep.

So before I let you go.

Know that I truly love you – infinitely.

Michelle Jean

Good God, good morning and good night.

Truly go back to bed.

We both need our sleep – rest.

I've nagged you enough so truly take care until later when I once again fatigue and nag you some more.

Truly thank you for staying awake with me. So smile because I am smiling. Hence the smile on my face.

Rest now my love – truly rest because you know now truly nagging I can be.

Snore if you have to because I know I will.

Truly take good care until I write to you again.

Michelle Jean
September 10, 2013

Good morning Good God it's me again.

Wow because it's 3:48 a.m.

God America is going to crumble and crumble big time.

I've seen the destruction of man. This destruction is before 2032.

This date is confirmed yet again.

Woooo Nelly America is going down and they are going to fall hard.

I did not see war Good God. It was as if the Washington Monument turned black and it just crumbled to the ground. All I saw was it coming down. God – Good God the monument was black. Wow. This fall is going to affect Canada as well.

Good God I so do not know how to describe it because the highways of Canada were packed with people trying to escape.

Good God I need to be on your bus – your good bus and or plane because the destruction of America does not look pretty.

God – Good God Babylon has and have fallen. I saw it.

I saw the destruction of humanity.
Wow

Truly woe be unto man because the first woe has sounded and humanity hath not a prayer for the sins they have done daily.

Good God the belly of the beast is no more – will be no more real soon.

All the feasting that they do will be over in a little while – shortly.

Woe be unto man when the second trumpet has sounded.

Truly woe be unto man because none will believe me when it comes to the destruction of man – humanity.

I did tell.

I feel sorry for no one because we all know the sins we have done.

Michelle Jean
September 11, 2013

Dear God – Good God have mercy and please do not let me get caught up in this rapture because America has crumbled.

Please do not let my family be caught up in the destruction of America.

Dear God nothing can save America from their pending doom.

Dear God Wow.

I did not see war just the monument coming down.

The monument was black and it came crashing down hard.

The monument was like a silo. Something you stored wheat – dry food in.

Good God no one was expecting this sudden fall.

Good God there goes the American economy.

Michelle Jean

Good God wow. The collapse of man – humanity.

Global economic collapse. Now the rich man is going to be like the poor man literally.

Doom and gloom.

The rich man will lose it all hence the woes of man – humanity will be heard globally.

Have mercy on my soul Good God because the earth will not be the same.

Allelujah remember Babylon System by Bob Marley?

He said, they graduated thieves and murderers. Bob Marley, Peter Tosh including Marcus Mosiah Garvey did tell. Now the first woe has sounded literally and truly woe be unto man.

Michelle Jean

Good God I am crying out to you hence truly help me and my family not to be in this country when all comes crashing down.

Please Good God find a safe haven for us because like I said, the fall of America is going to affect Canada.

Yes I was on the bus to Mississauga but I need more than that Good God. I need to be out of Canada safe and secure before the collapse of America.

Good God its early morn and I cannot go back to sleep.

Who do I warn because America is truly going down?

This I saw this morning. Truly woe be unto man.

Good God humanity may think this a joke but it's not a joke. It is real. You are showing me what's to take place real soon. This is the reality of man – humanity Good God. Hell will be on earth once America crumbles. But in all that I saw, I did not see the Chinese economy or land crumbling.

All I saw was the Washington Monument in black tumbling down to the ground.

God – Good God I do not know what or where or even how France came into play hence I am going to leave this alone because I am unsure of France.

I still remember the 3 flags side by side, The Canadian Flag, the French Flag and the Jamaican Flag. I do not know the meaning and I have to wonder if this is the order of the fall of these countries.

I truly do not know Good God because I just saw the fall of man – humanity and it's so not pretty. I do not know the global scale of this fall will be but it's before 2032.
Michelle Jean

Good God I see things hence I am going to leave man – humanity alone because it will be like Noah's Ark all over again. But this time it will be on a global scale.

God – Good God please let me truly find a good home in another land – South Africa preferably before all of the madness start.

If that place is South Africa Good God let me find a good home there now so that I can flee the madness that is to come. I need to flee with family – our family.

Good God from barren lands to fallen empires. Wow.

Hey I did see the smoke reaching beyond the heavens. Hence the fire is coming and truly woe be unto man.

Tell me Good God. Who is man going to blame this time around? They cannot blame you. They can only blame self because "THE WAGES OF SIN IS TRULY DEATH."

Michelle Jean

Yes Good God its early morn and I cannot sleep because of the dream I just had.

Good God wake up.
I'm waking you.

I saw the fall of America and it was not pretty.

God – Good God, I feel it in my stomach but not severely because America knew what they were doing. They knew this was coming. <u>Remember they rejected Marcus Mosiah Garvey hence they rejected you.</u>

To them Marcus Garvey could not be from you because he was black. Tell me Good God what other nation apart from Black People have you used to deliver your message?

You did try to help them (America) but they would not listen. Now I've seen the Washington Monument come a tumbling down.

Their economy is ruined hence many lands will cry because the beast would have taken them down with him. Hence the doom of America, the modern day seat of Babylon.

Michelle Jean

Good God lately the body is becoming over heated.

My body temperature is hot and it takes a while for the fan to cool it down.

God – Good God what's going on with my body?

What's happening to me with this heat – rising temperature?

It's like my body has become the sun – a furnace. It's truly overheating.

What's up with that?

Wow Good God my body is weird and I cannot take the heat of it.

Can you please direct my hormones and tell it to calm down they are moving too fast.

Tell them (my hormones) to cool down because my body is not hell.

I don't know Good God because the hormonal clock seem to be out of balance. We need to rescue it and put it back in check.

Good God I truly need this because like I said, my body is overheating and I cannot take the heat.

God – Good God it's not like hot flashes. When the heat comes it stays for awhile.

It's like my body cannot cool down. A fever does not describe it because I am hotter than that.

It's weird. Ah well maybe it's just me.

Maybe it's my mind but I know it's not my mind because right now I am sweating on the forehead.

Good God what is causing my body to overheat? The heat is annoying because I feel like I am dying sometimes but not all the time. It's like the heart rate has dropped. Weird but that's me. Too many pills – health woes.

Michelle Jean

Good God wake up because I so do not feel good in myself.

My spirit is not right and I don't know if it's because of my dream or what I am writing to you.

I don't know if I am scared but I truly need you to hold my hand. I truly need you to hold on to me.

I truly need you to be there for me.

God – Good God I am truly scared.

I am scared Good God because I do not know what's going to happen to me and my family.

Maybe it's me but I truly need your reassurance and your true protection.

I need you to be truly there for me and my family including the seeds – the good seeds you have given me.

Yes I know the harvest is here and truly woe be unto man.

No happiness will be on the faces of humanity – man.

No hope will billions have because they've given their lives over to the devil – death.

Good God prepare your children now and truly let them flee the belly of the beast before America comes tumbling down.

Michelle Jean

God – Good God wake up and be with me on this day because I am scared.

Hear me and ease my fright – pain.

I so don't want to be in North America when America goes down. Please find a good place for me and our family.

God – Good God I need you to hold my hand.

I need to be secure and happy with you.

I need your reassurance on this day that everything is going to be okay with us – our family.

I need guidance Good God as to what to do because the flood gates of sorrow will be opened soon and truly woe be unto man literally.

Good God in all that is going to happen and unfold, let me and our family find happiness, safety, your protection and safety, your blessings and truth in all of this.

Good God truly hold on to us and never let anyone of us fail you.

Do not let us go whatever you do.

Good God you are my true rose hence I come to you. Even nag you.

Good God truly be my good guide and hope because I truly do not want or need to lose you.

You are my everything, hence I am scared. Truly scared of what's to come.

I know you've never failed me but I have to tell you the truth.

I am truly scared.

Michelle Jean

Good God I've told you my fears and I am going to go back to bed.

The body is hot so I need to turn on back the fan.

I won't keep you away like yesterday. So truly thank you for waking up and hearing my fears – woes.

Many things are yet to come hence I've seen many lands barren. In my eyes Good God they are many because lands are going to split apart. I've seen this vision. It's only a matter of when.

Good God all that is to happen I will leave alone. Like I said, I am scared but I am depending on you to ease my fright.

<u>The mood – spirit is different. I don't know if there's a great lie that is to come into play. But I know there's a great lie somewhere is coming. I can feel it hence my fear is heightened. You Good God know the lie because</u>

you are further in the future and in time I know you will show me the lie. I don't know if humanity is going to denounce me but it matters not to me as long as you are truly on my side and by my side. I don't know what this lie is, but I am trusting you to defend and protect me as well as our good people.

Listen Good God, I cannot worry or think about what humanity thinks of me. At the end of the day I did your bidding and delivered your messages to the best of my ability.

If humanity want to continue to stray and say I'm a fraud then so be it because I am infinitely not the one residing outside of your garden and ark.

Like I said, I did what you required of me. I did write you books hence I obeyed you but I cannot say much for man – humanity.

Michelle Jean

Good God as long as I am not too late with you I am fine.

As long as we are on the same accord I am fine.

As long as we are true to each other then I am infinitely fine.

As long as we are good to each other I am fine.

As long as we truly infinitely truly love each other in truth in the flesh and spirit I am fine.

Good God you are fine by me hence I have to be fine by you.

I have to go back to bed now and I truly thank you for staying up with me for yet another night.

Yes I will nag you later because I so need my BBJ or a Gulfstream 550 so we can fly away together and be at true peace with each other.

Michelle Jean

Good God I have to go so see you later because the body temperature is rising yet again.

My body is hot and I need you to help me to balance out my hormones.

I don't know Good God but did you have to create so much heat in my body?

Man if only I could go to bed naked but I can't. I do not have a room all to myself. I'm sleeping in the living room on my sofa. Yes this is the way I need it because my daughter is too messy and I so don't want to share a bed or a room with her.

Soon I'll have my own room and yes I will go butt naked to bed.

Michelle Jean

Good God its 3:29 a.m. and I am up again hopefully not for long.

Good God I see the snakes. I know there are more deaths to come. The snakes are just roaming. Where they will hit in America is another story.

It's coming up to the end of the year and death must walk on land in America.

Their economy is going to fall and fall hard – huge but what is to be must be. The snake has nothing to do with the economy. There will be another mass killing this I know if my dream goes correctly.

Many will lose it all because it was ordained to be.

I cannot worry about America. I have to worry about me and you because like I said, they did reject your messenger Marcus Mosiah Garvey long ago and now this; their ruined economy.

I have to face reality. I truly have to prepare because this massive fall is going to affect Canada and the Canadian economy.

Good God truly save me from what is to come literally.

Remember I did see war. America going to war but this time, in this dream Aries was not on the battlefield with them. I did not see war; I saw the darkness – the blackness of the Washington Monument come tumbling down. Hence I say it's their economy that is going to crumble – tumble.

The blackness of the monument is not good. Before devastation hits you see blackness and I did see the blackness and woe be unto them.

Dear God and Good God maybe someone can decipher the dream for me but the dream did scare me.

I know this dream is in this lifetime. The time of their current president and although I did not see him I know he was there.

Good God many people are going to lose it all when the economy crumble hence you have to warn the people – prepare them for what's to come.

Remember I failed with hurricane Sandy and with the young lady that gave me the cure for AIDS. Please do not let me fail with this dream. Hurricane Sandy did her damage and this fall will do a greater damage because this was a huge fall. And like I said the fall did affect Canada.

Good God, I truly do not know what the Monument represents hence I assume it's the US economy. I know we are not to assume but in this case it cannot be helped.

Michelle Jean

Good God what is to be must be hence I am writing to you.

I truly need a vacation Good God hence I am waiting on your BBJ or Gulfstream 550.

Good God I truly need you. I need you to be with me because I saw the snakes hence please deliver me from harm's way.

The massive attack on the young is gearing up again. This I know because the snakes are looking for a place. Good God it's a matter of where because this time I saw an old sofa.

Please do not let the snakes come into my home because I would truly not be pleased.

I don't know if the target is old people because of the old sofa but something is going to go down.

You see and know all Good God hence America will not be the same.

Many lives will be lost hence man – humanity will know the true meaning of the wages of sins.

Once America falls this part of revelations will be complete.

The harlot would have truly done her job and humanity will have hell to pay.

Man will be looking for jobs and there will be none.

Families will shatter and scatter. No money to buy food.

1313 is almost here and truly woe be unto man and the global economy of mass and massive greed because the wealthy will become like the poor man. He too will be trying to find food to eat.

Michelle Jean

Good God it's early in the morning and I cannot worry about the devil's own.

I have to worry about me and you. I have to worry about our family.

Good God I have to worry about our sanity because the time of sin is truly winding down. Good God no weapon (s) formed against you and me including your people shall prosper hence the kingdoms of Satan must come crumbling down in a harsh and devastating way.

I have to warn now Good God so truly listen to me and help me in a good and true way.

I cannot change the past but we can prepare for the future. It's harvest time Good God and we have to store up good food including store up you and your goodness.

Yes Babylon is falling – infinitely going to fall because I saw it. I dreamt it. You showed it to me. Babylon your kingdom is falling and woe be unto you and your people because you are doomed.

Good God the great beast must fall and is falling because they've done all that is wicked and evil in thy sight.

They joined the devil to deceive man – humanity. Now they must pay and pay dearly. Hence they are going to come crashing down.

Prepare, prepare the great beast – Babylon is wounded. Prepare, Prepare and go tell ye lands – the people that the beast has been wounded. Babylon is falling thus saith/sayeth the Lord thy God meaning it is so. Prophesy now ye people. The time is at hand when you will see the great beast of old fall right before your eyes.

Prepare, prepare, you have to prepare all ye people of earth. You have to save yourself. You are being told now listen and save yourself from financial ruin.

Good God you have to prepare your people from financial ruin and starvation.

You have to help your people and let them flee from the destruction of evil – Babylon that great beast of old.

You cannot let your good people get caught up in all of this.

There is nor will there be any repentance anymore because for the wicked Aries must fall – was ordained to fall long ago.

Gather around all ye people.

That great beast has fallen. It has been wounded and woe be unto man – humanity – the economies of the earth.

Many will tumble with Babylon because they feasted with the harlot and the beast on the flesh of man – humanity and truly woe be unto them all.

Michelle Jean

It is a blessed Good Morning Good God. Truly wake up and dine with me because the great beast – Babylon is falling. It's going to come crashing – tumbling down.

Sit by my side and tell me you truly love me Good God.

Prepare your children now Good God because Babylon – America is set to fall. Has been ordained and commissioned to fall. It is only a matter of time when physical time catches up to spiritual time and Babylon comes a tumbling down.

The now president did not do his job. He turned from you and became one of the devil's own and he too must fall because he disobeyed you.

You ordained him to fix but instead of fixing he went to war. Because of this, Babylon must fall – will fall because death commissioned them – wants his massive pay day.

Death, death, death of many; economy in utter ruin for so many. Soon there will be no food to eat.

Barren lands, barren lands yes a few. For some food shortage, water shortage will be the cry shortly.

Man will truly feast on the flesh of man hence the scorpion kings of their holy bible.

Sin will feast
Death will walk
He will talk
Surely take

He will and must take what belongs to him and that is in the form of man's economy – his physical soul – flesh.

All the building and cheating that we do. We forgot about the wages of sin and that is death. The death of man humanity.

We forgot about the future of our children.

We forgot about our soul.
We forgot about our spirit.
We forgot about life – good and true life.
We forgot about you Good God.

We forgot that all that Satan gave he took back, hence leaving many in financial ruin – poverty – nothing.

Humanity forgot Satan was not stable. He cannot give that which he don't got – have. Hence he is SODOM – the true Sodom of the world. He is Gomorrah because he is linked and aligned with sin and death.

Yes he feasted on the flesh of man. He drove the economy of many into financial ruin – hell.

Yes man did forget the lies of Satan – Melchesidec – the ancient beast of old – the true deceiver – ultimate death – weaver of death.

Michelle Jean

Blessing and Peace be unto you Good God.

Blessing and Peace be unto you.

The fall of man has been ordained and there is nothing humanity can do to stop it.

1313, 2032, 2132 were the dates given to me. Hence 1313 is almost here and woe be unto man – humanity.

2132 we lost. How I truly do not know but many nations will fall – be left in utter ruin.

They must crumble – be lost.

Many cries will be heard globally but Good God, let there be true peace and blessings between me and you, our good and true family – people.

Peace and Blessings be unto you Good God.

Peace and Blessings be unto you.

You are my hope and guide. Truly take your people now out of the belly of the beast.

Peace and Blessings be unto you Good God.

Peace and Blessings be unto you.

Surround me always with your good and true love.

Secure me
Secure my children who are our children
Secure the good seeds you have given me.
Secure your good and true forever ever people.

Secure the land and lands you have given me. Hence truly SECURE SOUTH AFRICA – THE WOMB OF MOTHER – MOTHER AFRICA.

Secure the waters and food of Mama Africa.

Secure our true peace and sanity so that we will never ever forever ever never fall again or stray from your side.

Cover up and wrap us up securely in your good and true peace – your good and truly loving protective arms.

Let us fly away with you to the South – South Africa Good God.

Let us now build the South in truth – the truth of thee.

Let us build South Africa in a true and good way Good God.

Peace and Blessings be unto you Good God. You are All – Allelujah and I truly thank you. Bless you with all my goodness – my true and good heart.

Michelle Jean
September 12, 2013

Good God I do not know what to make of this dream hence I am so coming to you.

This dream had to do with Russia but I am leery and skeptical or Russia. Although the dream was odd, beautiful, something is just not right. I don't know if I should include this dream in this book but I am going to anyway. It is a long dream so here goes.

It was as if I was in Russia. The setting was nice as if it was winter but there was no snow.

Good God I came across a tree. A huge tree. The tree was tall as a mango tree but it was not mangoes on the tree it was strawberries. Good God when I say strawberries I mean strawberries. The tree was packed with Strawberries. Good God you know I touched on Russia in Blackman Redemption the Death of Russia. I know they hate my ass but I had to touch on them given what was shown to me. Hence I am warning Russia because if they think you Good God is dicking around with them they had better think again. They will end up like the United States and come crumbling down hence the dream I've had about them prior to this one.

<u>I am tired of the nonsense Good God and I cannot comprehend nor over stand and understand why humanity refuses to listen.</u>

<u>This is harvest time and none will listen but like I said, I've delivered the messages you have given me to give to these lands.</u>

You nor I failed them, they failed you and self. Yes I tried to warn America before hurricane Sandy hit land but the person I sent the book to never read the cover. I did try but failed in my doing hence this time I am giving more notice. <u>If the people of America ignore me – the message and not prepare financially and economically for this fall, then none can blame me or you because they were told.</u>

They failed to listen yet again. Because if they had truly listened to Marcus Mosiah Garvey when it came to economics then none of this would happen, meaning America would not have such a massive debt. The land would be saved but because he Marcus Mosiah Garvey did not fit America's portfolio of a messenger because he was BLACK they rejected him hence rejecting you and your message.

He Marcus Garvey was preparing the people of America for the BACK TO AFRICA MOVEMENT and it did not pan out but TODAY, THEY HAVE TO PREPARE AND GO BACK TO AFRICA, SOUTH AFRICA WHICH IS THE WOMB.

They must return home and they have to do it now lest they will get caught up in this massive rapture – harvest that is to come. Hence I AM WARNING SOUTH AFRICA TO KNOW YOUR PEOPLE GOOD GOD. South Africa and the Southern lands of Africa cannot take in any and anyone into their good lands Good God and this is where I need you to intervene. **You cannot under any circumstances allow the devil's children to flee to this land. I am trusting you to keep them (the devil's children) at bay. Keep them the hell out of South Africa and the Southern land and lands of Africa.**

Also, I need you to infinitely and truly evict the devil's own from your good land and lands. I refuse to reside with the devil's own because they have nothing to do with me and you. I refuse to have them come into the land and lands of the Mother Land – Mother Africa and destroy it. I refuse to help you clean up Africa – MY MOTHER'S LAND and have them come back in and or stay and destroy it. I will not have it because like I said, I need to abide by you and enjoy you. I need you in all that I do.

ONWARDS I GO.

Like I said, the strawberry tree was packed –filled with strawberries. They were ripe. I was bewildered in a way because it was winter but no snow was on the ground and the strawberry tree had so many strawberries on it. Good God I've never seen so many strawberries on a tree before. Strawberries do not grow on such a tall tree Good God we all know this.

Anyway, this singer from the group N Sync no before he came I picked some of the strawberries by using a rock and throwing it in the tree. The strawberries I got – caught where bad – no good. I could not eat them. Even when I squeezed them I could not eat them they were rotten. For some strange reason there were ripe tomatoes and the same thing was with the tomatoes. No I did not pick the tomatoes it was if I got them in my hand and when I squeezed it (them) it too was rotten, weird I know. So the squeeze I was squeezing one of the members of N Sync climbed the strawberry tree with ease and began to pick the strawberries. Suffice it to say I got some good strawberries and I did eat. I don't know this dream is weird because his manager who was black in the dream came and began to talk to us. Him especially because he had a concert to do but I did not get a ticket. He did not have one for me. I wanted to talk to him more because for some strange reason I wanted him to be my manager and take on the soliciting of my books but it did not pan out we had to leave. See this dream had to do with stealing because it was like the member of N Sync was stealing the strawberries. I was taken to this place and once again it involved an American, an American actress – she was young. One of the members of the television show Zoey 101. She was in Russia and she was stealing clothes and jewelry. Everything she could get her hand on she was stealing it. Trust me I don't know how I got one of her bags but one of her bags with some of the things she stole I had in my hand. She stole this afghan sweater – an exact replica of one that a well to do person was wearing. I saw the sweater on the person and she had a pink one on and I said you stole that. She did not say anything. She just kept walking hence she got away.

After all that drama went down because in her apartment – where she was staying was messy. Everything in the apartment was stolen.

Coming to the end of the dream we were in a department store and everything was nice and clean – high end. It was in the department store I told her she stole the sweater and she kept walking. Like I said, the sweater was pink and it fit like a dress. I know pink is very good in a dream hence she got away with the theft.

I went over to where they sold body wash and I saw this pretty bottle with a nice fragrant body wash and I picked it up to buy it because I could not believe Russia had such beautiful bottles of body wash. Now the weird part is Prokhorov found me in the department store. Hugged me, kissed me on the lips and said he wanted to marry me and I woke up out of my sleep. It was freaking weird to have him kiss me hence I call that the kiss of death and the marriage of death in reality.

Weird dream hence I am going to leave it alone because **someone is stealing from Russia and they don't even know it.**

To me their good deed was a planted deed. There to steal information from them in the most elegant of way and he is stealing and they just don't know it because the dream entailed American's stealing from Russia not the other way around.

So Russia whether you like me or not this is what I saw and you can hate me all you want. Your strawberries are full and ripe but they were rotten to the core hence someone or something stinks in Russia and you have to find it and clean up your strawberry and tomato trees. Your goodness is being stolen from you hence *you have to overhaul your security system.*

You have a rogue in your midst hence the stealing of vital security information from you.

You now have your dream. Use it and decipher it wisely because YOU ARE TRULY BEING DECEIVED AND YOU JUST DON'T KNOW IT. WELL NOW YOU KNOW SO TRULY GUARD YOUR DEFENCES – RUSSIAN SECURITY or whatever you need to guard because like I said, you are being deceived and in the dream American's are stealing from you. You must know what you have for them to steal hence truly good luck because I did see Russia casting its net (hose) to get oil and yielding nothing. Good God is trying to tell you something so truly listen because at the end of the day America is going to fall – come crashing down and if you are not careful you will fall alongside them.

Michelle Jean

ONWARDS I GO GOOD GOD because I've delivered your message. It's up to Russia now to act because it's not right for another man and or country to set up another land and steal from them. Hence America is going to fall and fall hard. What they are doing is wrong. Come on now Good God.

America must fall because of their deceit hence I told you Good God about the great lie.

There is a great lie somewhere and I infinitely know what's done in the dark must come to light.

Like I said, I don't care if Russia don't like me but they have to do better. This is their economy and people and you are trying to warn them. America did not listen to Marcus Mosiah Garvey but I am asking you to let Russia truly listen. **The ancients of their land need them to listen and not end up like America.** They have the one **RIPE MANGO AND IF THEY DON'T USE THE ONE RIPE MANGO WISELY AND TAKE HEED THEIR LAND WILL BECOME BARREN AND NO ONE CAN BLAME YOU OR ME GOOD GOD BECAUSE THE**

MESSAGE WAS DELIVERED IN A GOOD AND TRUE WAY.

Trust me I will not feel sorry for them if they don't listen because like I said, I saw the Washington Monument in black looking like a silo come a tumbling – crashing down.

The tumble this monument came tumbling down did affect Canada. Like I said, I do not know the role France played or what France had to do with this dream but they France were involved.

No France did not tumble America's economy. The fall of America affected them in some way.

Like I said, I saw the Canadian Flag, the French Flag and the Jamaican Flag side by side and I still do not know what to make of it. If someone knows please tell the world know because I cannot put these three flags together. And for those that are going to ask when this tumble is going to take place. It is before 2032. Your current president was involved in this dream hence I say shortly this will happen. I did not see him but he was involved.

This dream did not entail water, so I cannot say within the next three to nine months.

Dreams that involve water is easy to decipher but dry dreams that entail no water I cannot truly give a time line.

They take longer to come to pass hence you all still have time to prepare yourself financially I hope.

<u>I have to say I hope because like I said, I did not see water but keep in mind 1313, 2032 and 2132. Correlate them to the dates of Daniel because he too was given dates. I cannot put them together for you because I truly do not know how to nor do I want to know how to either.</u>

Canadians also have to prepare because like I said, this dream affected them.

I have delivered the message so please listen and truly take heed. Guard yourself as to what's to come. There are no ands ifs or buts about this fall because like I've told you in another book, I did see **<u>WHITE AND BLACK DEATH TOGETHER AND ONE HAD THE SCROLL OF DEATH IN HIS HAND.</u>** *Hence truly woe be unto man because the death sentence in the physical and spiritual has and have been ordained.* **<u>Death must come. Death must be carried out.</u>**

<u>Both deaths were together like I said, hence man will die in the physical and spiritual right away.</u>

Many are going to be looking for a prayer and none will be given because of the sins of man – the sins we do on a daily basis.

My homeland will be destroyed because Good God told me my homeland is unclean.

I know Jamaica is going to come back to but like I said, one tried to set me up. Yes this is a dream hence I tell Good God I will not beg for any of my people in Jamaica because I know the hearts and minds of my own people. It is not clean but unclean, so I have to leave them the people of Jamaica to their own destruction.

Like I said, Good God told me that Jamaica is unclean and he showed me my set up once the land has been cleaned and like I said, I leave my own people to their own downfall.

<u>Also, because Jamaica has been deemed unclean by Good God, no land can take Jamaicans directly from Jamaica into their land or lands lest they become unclean also.</u>

No one can vacation in the land lest they become unclean also.

Trust me this has nothing to do with me. It has to do with you and staying clean and true to God – Good God, because this harvest is going to be brutal.

<u>If you go to Jamaica you risk your own death. Because you were told Jamaica is unclean. And by you going into the land, you will be like Eve (Evening) and you must be ejected from Good God's world</u>

and kingdom because you willingly disobeyed his word.

Yes I want to go back for a vacation by I cannot go and I am going to leave it at that.

So no human being or country can say, "but God – Good God you did not warn me." YOU WERE WARNED HENCE THIS BOOK AND THE EMAILS I WILL NOT SEND OUT TO WARN HUMANITY.

MICHELLE JEAN

Ah my True Love and God. Please join me.

Please be my guide in all that I do.

You are Good Life hence I present to you, truth, good tidings, good cheer, good laughter, good people, good all – good everything.

You are peace
True love
My one accord

You are time
Beyond time

You are African – South Africa
You are Black, Green and Gold including Blue – Light Blue and White.

You are Jamaican, the Mother Land – Africa.

You are free
Good will
Good all
You are Good God and I truly infinitely truly, truly love you.

Michelle Jean

Good God and friend a blessed and good morning to you.

Yes it's our morning date and I just want to say I truly love you and hope you truly love me.

Michelle Jean

Keep me close in thine heart Good God. Please keep me close.

It's early morn now and I must go back to bed.

You are my stay
My keep
My all

I truly love you because you are my one and all.

Michelle Jean

*In thee do I put my trust Good God.
In thee do I put my trust.*

*Be my good fly – airplane at all times.
Be my good wings and eyes. The good and perfect jet fuel that gets me from point A to point B.*

*Be my good pilot
My good all
Be my good Butler
My good and clean Baker
My good and clean Doctor
My good and clean Chef – Meal Maker – Preparer*

Good God be my good and appropriate clothes that I wear.

Be my good and nappy hair.
Be my good eyes to see.
Be my good food that I eat.

By my good drinks that I drink including my good and clean water and air.
Good God truly be my good all.

Michelle Jean

Good God it's after four am in the morning. I truly need your private jet so that I can jet away.

I truly need your BBJ if not your Gulfstream 550.

Good God I truly need to fly.
I truly need to get away from all this madness that is to come.

Good God, I truly need to write the New Book of Life – Life.

Good God let's fly away together. We can take our good and true people with us.

Good God we truly need to escape this madness – harvest that is to come.

Michelle Jean
September 12, 2013

Good God this morning I don't want to sleep. I just want to meditate on you.

I need to focus on you and let you be the attention in my good life.

Good God let me behold you yet again.
Let me behold your true and good beauty.

Let's hold hands.
Walk side by side in glory.

Good God you are my darling.
My true friend.
My true one and all.
My true one and only.

Be at true peace with me my true love.
Truly rest with me for a little while.

Know that I truly love you.
I give you true and good thanks for all you've done for me and my family.

Michelle Jean

Good God I am getting tired so I have to bid you good morning.

Please have a coffee for me.

No I am not sleepy, just want to meditate on you but I truly don't know how to. You know my mind. It will go all over the place to keep me from truly meditating on you after a while.

My spirit cannot stay truly focused on you in thought. I have to write hence thoughts are not for me truly.

Good God you know that when I get to South Africa we have to do this each and every morning.

Good God I still need our early morning wake up calls.

I truly need to communicate with thee.

So for me and you. Find that perfect and good place for me and you so that we can be together forever ever infinitely and indefinitely.

Yes if possible beside the river of water – a nice waterfall because I truly need to be with you. Be truly near you.

Good God we cannot leave each other's sight because I am truly with you and you are truly with me.

We are each other's protector and true love. Good blessings. Besides Good God you more than infinitely know that I cannot be without you because **you truly and infinitely complete me.**

You are my good rain and cool air – my true breath of life.

So truly hold on to me as I hold on to you in peace and true and good blessings. Peace, true peace and blessings be unto you until I truly wake you again with all my true love and thoughts.

Michelle Jean
September 12, 2013

OTHER BOOKS BY MICHELLE JEAN

MY NAGGING DAY
BLACKMAN REDEMPTION – THE DEATH OF RUSSIA
A DIFFRENT MOOD AND WORLD – THINKING

THE NEW BOOK OF LIFE – ME
THE NEW BOOK OF LIFE – JUDGEMENT
THE NEW BOOK OF LIFE
THE NEW BOOK OF LIFE – A CRY FOR THE CHILDREN

THE DAYS I AM WEAK
CRAZY THOUGHTS – MY BOOK OF SIN
JUST ONE OF THOSE DAYS – BOOKS 1 – 4
ODE TO MR. DEAN FRASER

BLACKMAN REDEMPTION
 A LITTLE LITTLE TALK
PRAYERS
MY COLLECTIVE

A LITTLE TALK/ A TIME FOR FUN AND PLAY
SIMPLE POEMS
BEHIND THE SCARS
LOVE BOUND
LOVE BOUND BOOK TWO

SONGS OF LOVE AND PRAISE
DEDICATION UNTO MY KIDS
MORE TALK
SAVING AMERICA FROM A WOMAN'S PERSPECTIVE

MY COLLECTIVE – THE DARK SIDE OF ME
A BLESSED DAY

BLACKMAN REDEMPTION – THE WAR OF ISREAL
BLACKMAN REDEMPTION – THE WAY I SPEAK TO GOD
BLACKMAN REDEMPTION – A LITTLE TALK WITH MAN
BLACKMAN REDEMPTION – THE DEN OF THIEVES
BLACKMAN REDEMPTION – THE DEATH OF JAMAICA

BLACKMAN REDEMPTION – HAPPY MOTHER'S DAY
LOSE TO WIN
MY DOUBTFUL DAYS – BOOK ONE

BLACKMAN REDEMPTION – THE DEATH OF FAITH
MY LITTLE TALK WITH GOD
MY LITTLE TALK WITH GOD – BOOK TWO

BLACKMAN REDEMPTION – THE WAR OF RELIGION